Praise for *Brand Buzz* and Adrienne Weiss Corporation

"Adrienne Weiss was an extraordinary branding partner. She translated what I saw in my head to a global brand that exceeded even my wildest expectations. Every time I walk by one of our bright and cheery stores (color scheme her idea) and see the kids and kids at heart having the time of their lives, I thank my lucky stars for Adrienne Weiss and her team."

—*Maxine Clark, Founder and Chairman of Build-A-Bear Workshop*

"Over my career, I have faced several serious brand transformations. In every case, when the strategy discussion started relating to the essential brand changes…Adrienne Weiss was at the table with me… Her insights were invaluable…and right on target. It is no coincidence that these successful brand shifts had Adrienne's imprint. The transformations couldn't have been accomplished without her 'brand brilliance.'"

—*Jon Luther, former CEO and Chairman of Dunkin' Brands Group, Inc., former President of Popeye's Louisiana Kitchen, Inc., and Chairman of Arby's Restaurant Group, Inc.*

"I've worked with Adrienne Weiss for over twenty years, and I feel she's a genius in brand marketing. She has the ability to simply zero in on a problem and create an amazing solution. Adrienne is a joy to work with and an authentic talent!"

—*Richard Melman, Founder and Chairman of Lettuce Entertain You Enterprises, Inc.*

"Adrienne Weiss is a living legend in the world of branding! She clearly sees, 'the forest through the trees,' when it comes to retail, design, packaging, and presentation!"

—*Dan Romanelli, former President of Warner Bros. Consumer Products*

BRAND™
buzz

3 Breakthrough Secrets
for Building a Winning Brand

adrienne weiss • greg weiss

simple ▶ truths®
small books. **BIG IMPACT.**

Photo Credits: Adrienne Weiss Corporation

Published by Simple Truths, an imprint of Sourcebooks, Inc.
P.O. Box 4410, Naperville, Illinois 60567–4410
(630) 961-3900
Fax: (630) 961-2168
www.sourcebooks.com

Printed and bound in China.
QL 10 9 8 7 6 5 4 3 2 1

Dedicated to Esther Weiss

Adrienne Weiss Corporation is a three-generation family business. This is a sweet and powerful thing in America. We would like to dedicate this book to our founding partner Esther Weiss, who thirty years ago, at the age of seventy, began her career as CFO for our start-up. She brought wisdom, humor, steadiness, and confidence to the tender first days of our company, and she later brought her savvy skills at finance to keep us fueled. She worked until her eighty-ninth year. Gregory and I only wish she could be here to witness and share this joyful moment of the birth of our book.

We would like to acknowledge the love and support of Keren, Ethan, Hannah, Amelia, and Lynne, our tribe in Chicago who encouraged and added to our imagination and energy to create this book. Thank you, all. We love you.

CONTENTS

Introduction

Good ideas are often a two-sided coin: one side emotional, the other side intellectual.

In the early days of branding, I stood on stages showing photos of cows with distinctive brand marks on their bellies and had to then go on to explain, "No, no, I don't mean this kind of branding."

Branding is the distinctive mark, message, and way of doing business that separates a business from its competitors and makes a lasting impression on its consumers. We've come a long way: from those days of single burn marks on cowskins to complex marks all over the bodies of world-class businesses.

In our thirty years of building brands in many industries all over the world, we have discovered a simple and straightforward way to create a better brand. Whether it is a start-up or a mature, multiunit business, these three steps lead to the ability to connect and engage with customers, patients, clients, guests, passengers, or fans in a way that builds a lasting relationship. In this book, you will learn how to unlock the secrets of building a winning brand that creates brand buzz.

There are buzzwords, building buzz, and feeling buzzed—but no matter which way you look at it, you want your brand to be about buzz. Buzzwords are shorthand for how your customer might want to talk about your brand. Building buzz is the result of continuing to tell your brand story in innovative ways. Feeling buzzed is when your product or service hits the culture in exactly the right way, and it turns into something that inspires or thrills. Brands that buzz are brands that people can't stop talking about and customers love to support.

You will no doubt notice that our book is equal measure words and pictures. It has been said that half the population is visual and the other half is verbal. In an effort to punctuate this point, and in the ancient tradition of storybooks, we are demonstrating that a story well told needs to be both visual and verbal. You will likely move between the words and pictures of this book to get the fullest understanding of our story, just as your guest or customer will move between these two expressions in your own brand to most fully engage with your business.

While *brand* and *branding* are buzzwords these days, there is a lot of confusion about what exactly building a winning brand entails. As brand experts and inventors of brands, we want to help you make your brand stand out and truly tell and sell who you are to your customers. We have worked with blank-slate start-ups, such as Build-A-Bear Workshop and Five Below, both of which were sketches on napkins when we started working with them and eventually became public companies. We have worked with mature and well-established brands, such as McDonald's and Coca-Cola. Regardless of the size, age, or reputation of your company, or your own personal brand for that matter, the important thing is not where you are starting; it is where you are going. If you encompass the three principals most important in creating a positive brand culture, you will always have your brand compass to lead you.

The importance of a brand should not be underestimated. The collective details of your business can be great, and your customer experience can be great, but without an overarching story, you will have trouble creating a strong and connective relationship with your customer. You need a big basket to hold everything together and create a common mission. When raising money with investors, when talking to the press, when forming a marketing plan, the one thing that often elevates, inspires, and creates momentum is the "vision."

We want to offer you the three secrets to help you build a better brand.

Branding, as you will read in the pages ahead, has three main components:

First, every truly great brand tells a great STORY. A brand can have an engaging logo, fashionable colors, and cool artwork, but if there is no core story—no emotional and intellectual anchor—then the customer will not have anything to hold on to. The news flash here is that the story is not a story about the business; it is a consumer-centric story answering the question "What's in it for me?"

Second, a brand creates the feeling of a CLUB that people want to be a part of. For a brand to be great, people must want to associate themselves with it. The brand must create a desire for affinity within its customer base.

Third, a great brand acts like a COUNTRY with its own language, ceremonies, and customs. A brand must have its own way of doing things—you want your customer to feel like Dorothy stepping out of black and white and into the brilliant color of Oz.

We use these three pillars to benchmark the true greatness of a brand and help companies create their own brilliant brands. Routinely, we find ourselves tasked with telling a company or team's story succinctly, artfully, and in a way that would capture the imagination of the public. In the stories in the pages ahead, we will cover the building of brands through these three pillars of storytelling, club making, and country building. Each company presented had unique circumstances that required unique, creative thought, but regardless of the industry or challenge faced, the process of building a brand remains the same.

Start with the details. Many times people do the big things first and then lose heart, time, or money when it's time to do the details. Guess what?!

the consumer's attention is in the details

Story-telling

On the south side of Chicago in the 1950s, my grandfather Ben Weiss created a shoe store called Cinderella Shoes. He employed the most literal way of crafting a brand story by taking a well-known and beloved fairy tale and putting that story's title right into his brand's name. By taking the story of Cinderella and borrowing the emotional and intellectual equity for its own, the promises of quality (glass slippers) and fashion rightness (even princes admired them) were brought to the customers of Cinderella Shoes. The brand was building a connection to its customers that the competition down the street could not. Cinderella Shoes illustrates the first of the three pillars of brand building: STORYTELLING.

A story is a collection of words, pictures, or actions that unfold in a compelling way. Stories come in many colors and themes. There are romantic stories, adventure stories, humorous stories, and very serious stories. We use

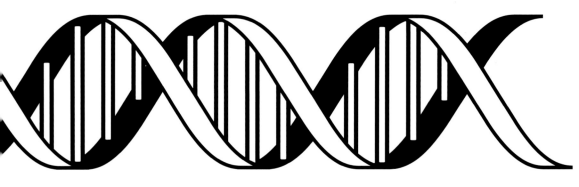

the word story to help you understand that it is the "unfolding" that is important. The idea of putting the same mark on every sign, package, or truck is not the same as revealing a story that builds on itself and is engaging over time.

The first step in creating a story is understanding your company's DNA. A great way of determining that is to look at your customers and answer the most important question that they will ask: *What's in it for me?* In the case of Build-A-Bear Workshop, that answer is friendship. In the case of LYFE Kitchen, that answer is food the consumer will love, food that is better for them, and a place where they have the power to choose their own food policy. In the case of Bissell, that answer is someone who knows what I need and how I can best clean my home. Your DNA is a reflection of what you do well and what your customer expects of you. When trying to determine your DNA, think about your connection to the world—your reason for existing. What is it that you do better than anyone else? Why is it that a customer will want to do business with you?

Once you understand what your brand story must communicate, then the tone must be set. Is your brand friendly? Is it authoritative? Is it hip? Is it sophisticated? Is it young? Is it mature?

If your brand is aspirational, it should have a look and feel that reflects where your customer is going, not where the customer is now. If your brand is democratic, it should look and feel as if everyone can join in and be a part of the movement.

The next step, and often the hardest, is filling out the rest of the story: the words and pictures that express your DNA. If your brand stands for caring and kindness, what are the words and pictures that express that? If it is about luxurious comfort, what are the symbols, colors, textures, sayings, and phrases that reflect that? This is where creative thinking is needed. A brand is both words AND pictures—a good tag line, a turn of phrase, or a well-placed pun must work with the right color or image on the side of a package or on the point of sale.

The final step is finding where you can leverage this story. What are your consumer touch points and how can you communicate through them? The key to this process is to walk in your customers' shoes and think about where they interact with your brand. They see the store, they open your shipping boxes, and they sit at your tables. These are all opportunities to communicate your brand story and send all decisions through your story filter.

MILLER PARK®/
HOME TO HEROES

"This is what I do, son."

When Miller Park opened in Milwaukee in 2001, it cost a whopping $400 million to build and was the largest construction project in the history of the state of Wisconsin. This presented a great opportunity to create not only a symbol of the highest ideal of sports, but at the same time to also create a world-class icon of civic pride. In order to achieve both these lofty goals, there needed to be an authentic story that could be told throughout the fan experience in the stadium.

The story would come to be "Home to Heroes." The heroes of the story were not just the great baseball players that had played in Milwaukee, including Hank Aaron, Robin Yount, and Paul Molitor, but the story would also include the hardworking men and women of the state of Wisconsin who gathered in this beautiful building to cheer on their team.

America loves baseball.

Nowhere is this more apparent than in Wisconsin.

Baseball has given sports some of its most inspired moments, becoming memorable parables illustrating America's unique strengths and unparalleled achievements.

Beneath the uniforms, behind the dugout, and throughout the bleachers are warriors, heroes, and ordinary, hardworking, fun-loving people who have something in common: a game called baseball in a place called Wisconsin.

Wisconsin's future is inextricably linked to the people who call it home. If not for its leaders, laborers, inventors, artists, visionaries, farmers, and athletes, it would not be the thriving center of learning, culture, industry, business, and recreation that it is today.

Miller Park is proud to celebrate the extraordinary achievements of the people we call heroes.

This story is told in a variety of ways throughout the park. It is told in an intimate, close-up format in print, both in the program and packaging. It is also told in a large-scale format in giant murals throughout the concourse that depict the various industries that help the state of Wisconsin thrive. These industries include tourism, paper manufacturing, dairy farming, and brewing, among other Wisconsin passions. The murals depict exciting baseball moments, and these are surrounded by images of people working within each one of these important Wisconsin industries. The intent was to create not just a building but a gathering place that is not only meaningful to Wisconsin, but could *only* exist there. Walking the concourse became an *experience*, a moment when a parent could stop and point to a piece of art and tell their child "That is what Mommy does" or "That is where Daddy works." **This is a story not just about a team, but a story also about the fans.**

A secondary benefit of this storytelling technique is that it created an innovative sponsorship strategy. The businesses that wanted to be associated with Wisconsin—Harley-Davidson, Wausau Paper, and others—could be integrated into the experience by hosting a piece of art. They achieved this by using their logos next to the murals rather than in a more traditional and less fluid manner, such as billboards around the stadium. In this way, sponsors could be a part of this beautiful building rather than detract from it.

The takeaway here is that your brand should incorporate the fan—this is not just a story about the heroes on the field, but it is a story about the heroes in the stands as well. Sports already have a tribal feeling—how often do you find yourself saying "We won last night" when talking about your favorite team? The story of Miller Park reinforces this connection and provides a clear framework to allow the sponsors to be a part of that story. Harley-Davidson is not just a great company with great products that wants to connect with the fans of the Brewers; they are a part of the rich fabric of Wisconsin, and therefore they feel at home advertising in the concourses of Miller Park. Put the fan, customer, or guest into your brand, into the story—this will help create a connection to your brand.

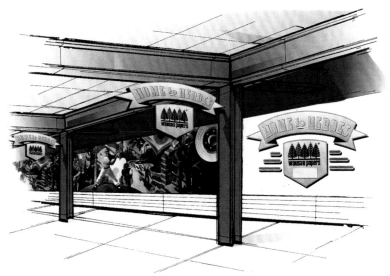

BASKIN-ROBBINS™

"Time to reSCOOPerate!"

Baskin-Robbins is a loved brand, but around the turn of the millennium, it was a brand that felt dated—sliding from nostalgic to tired. Founded in 1945, it had started as an innovator—offering an abundant thirty-one flavors—but as time passed, Baskin-Robbins became known as the old standby. Being a standby is certainly not the dynamic position of "innovator" that it held for over fifty years, and it would not lead them into the new millennium. At this point, fancy, upscale competitors began capturing market share. Baskin-Robbins was fading from the competitive landscape. The ice-cream world seemed to be moving toward fancy

flavors and exotic mix-ins—
think vanilla-curry ice cream
with Valrhona dark chocolate
chunks or coconut ice cream
infused with ginger and lime. What
began as a simple industry with
simple yet inventive flavors
for kids had evolved into
gourmet products designed for
sophisticated palates. The stores were
decorated in mahogany, brass, and marble. Kids,
fun, and family were quickly disappearing from ice
cream and its joyful simplicity.

There was a clear opportunity for Baskin-Robbins to

focus on its fifty-year history and strong brand equity and build a fun and relatable world around it. The first step was to create a new logo with strong, kid-friendly energy. The number 31 has always been a strong part of the Baskin-Robbins brand—it is a number that is only associated with Baskin-Robbins and communi-cates one of their brand strengths—variety. The number 31 is now directly embedded into the logo (look again, if you have not noticed it).

The second step for Baskin-Robbins was to bring the fun back to ice cream and create a fun, family-friendly environment. To that end, when you walk into a Baskin-Robbins, you are now surrounded by half-cartoon/half-retro-Americana art of people enjoying their ice cream. The characters are fun and unique, and the look is completely ownable by Baskin-Robbins. The artwork was created in such a way that it can be sliced and diced in any way necessary to fit the great variety of retail spaces throughout the Baskin franchise system. The messaging is built directly into the artwork, with sayings such as "freeze the day" and "time to reSCOOPerate" floating freely in the art. In some places, such as Korea, there are four-story BR Cafés with huge, blown-up characters filling the spaces.

The heart of the story here is that whatever your brand story is, you should own it and yell it out loud. Here, Baskin-Robbins found itself off trend. The trend was sophistication and that was not its strength—its strength was kid-friendly, fun ice cream that the whole family could enjoy. It took this strength, believed in its core competencies, and expressed its brand story clearly. A brand story is not something that is found on the outside; it exists within a company—finding it and expressing it in a consumer-friendly way is the true challenge.

IT'S NOT DELIVERY. IT'S DiGiorno.

DiGiorno.

MAMA MIA

NEW

YOUR KITCHEN'S A PIZZERIA

pizzeria!

artisan style crust · created with care

the crust!
crispy on
the outside,
soft & airy
on the inside
made with
extra virgin
olive oil

the sauce!
flavorful
sauce
made with
vine-ripened
tomatoes

the cheese!
premium
mozzarella,
aged
parmesan,
fontina &
pecorino
romano

the taste!
preservative
free crust
no artificial
flavors

SERVING SUGGESTION

quattro formaggi / four cheese pizza

DIGIORNO® PIZZERIA!™

"Mama mia! Your kitchen is a pizzeria!"

Have you ever walked the frozen pizza aisle at the supermarket? There are a lot of frozen pizza brands out there, and even those with well-developed brand stories need to differentiate themselves further for attention. DiGiorno, the best-developed brand in the industry, created a new product that tastes like an old-style pizzeria pizza with an artisan-style crust.

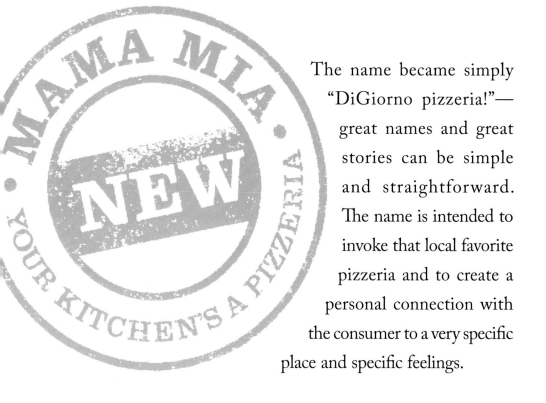

The name became simply "DiGiorno pizzeria!"—great names and great stories can be simple and straightforward. The name is intended to invoke that local favorite pizzeria and to create a personal connection with the consumer to a very specific place and specific feelings.

The packaging supports this idea of connecting the food to a place—the box looks like an old neighborhood pizzeria with brick walls, a concrete windowsill, and classic shutters. Even the shape of the box supports this story, with curved edges mimicking the shape of an awning hanging overhead. The feeling of eating DiGiorno pizzeria! puts you back in the old neighborhood. This is three-dimensional storytelling, packaging, placement, and product all express the same plot line.

foodli

be kind. eat true.

your sex life, without also thinking of your food life? A food court does not need a name, but an exciting eating experience certainly does. And that is how foodlife was born.

The communication within the four walls of the restaurant was not only about food, value, quality, and service; it was also about life. Rather than putting banners in the rafters that said "Order a taco" or "Best burgers in town," the banners

call your mother.

smile often.

had messages that said "Know right from wrong," "Every day counts," and "Call your mother." Rather than using the expanse of a large wall for artwork or wallpaper, the message "Do you know where you are on your journey?" was subtly painted in tiny lettering so that the guests had to stop and look and think about what they were reading rather than be hit over the head with it. The story that this brand told was not a story focused only on food at the end of the day, but a story focused on lifestyle, a way of living that was bigger than just the burgers and burritos that they served.

It can be helpful to think of your brand as more than just a product or a retail outlet or restaurant or entertainment center— think of it as a part of your customers' lives. The story that your brand tells must be about more than the qualities of your own product; it must tell a story about how it fits into your customers' lives. It is not just a matter of fit. Your brand story must feel as if your brand enhances, improves, and is indispensable to your guests' lives. The story must be timeless and universal.

some foodlife™ philosophy:

 be kind.

 eat true.

 learn stuff.

 wake up.

 act now.

corner

bakery™

you knead it.

CORNER BAKERY™

"I knead it daily."

Let them eat bread! Better yet, let them eat cherry chocolate bread or cheddar bread. This was at the heart of the inspiration for Corner Bakery. From its beginnings as a small, quality bakery adjacent to Maggiano's Little Italy restaurant to the monster chain it has become, Corner Bakery certainly proved that we all KNEAD bread. In order to create something bigger than a neighborhood bakery, it needed to have a culturally relevant story that had attitude and the promise of experience.

you only
knead a
few things
in life...

CIABATTA · BAGUETTE · FIG
HONEY WHEATBERRY · OLIVE
FOUGASSE · WALNUT · THYME
ITALIAN · DILL · RAISIN PECAN
RYE · CHOCOLATE CHERRY
COUNTRY SOURDOUGH · GARLIC
SESAME SEMOLINA · RAISIN
CORN RYE · RAISIN BRIOCHE
ROSEMARY & OLIVE OIL ·
OLIVE BATARD · FICELLE...

This was where the friendly little chef with a giant mitt and the rallying cry "YOU KNEAD IT!" was born. This filter drove all the creative decisions in building a chain. This was one story that unified everything. It was the front-of-the-house story reminding the guests that they knead bread with the suggestion that "you only knead a few things in life…rye, cherry, wheat…" It was also the story that was on the bakers' aprons: I KNEAD IT DAILY. This put the staff and the guests in the same world. It was a world of quality, smart humor, and lightheartedness.

We often say that if no one communicates the brand message in the trenches, then the consumer touch points would have to work on their own to be understood. The goal when designing the food packaging was to create something that someone would want to buy even if they had no idea what was in it. The goal with the employee uniforms was to make the employees part of the entertainment—make them a canvas for communicating the brand story by just walking around the store while doing their jobs. Take every opportunity you have to communicate the brand, and leverage it as well as you can. The idea of making employee T-shirts entertaining seems commonplace now, but this was a revolutionary idea when Corner Bakery first started. Find your underleveraged opportunities and turn the volume up!

i knead it daily.

BISSELL®

"Why be a carpet-cleaner manufacturer when you can be the authority on clean?"

Bissell was founded in 1876 and is one of the most well-known and trusted brands in the carpet-cleaning industry. Bissell is a true innovator in many ways; it not only invented the first "carpet sweeper," but it also had the first female CEO in the United States. Bissell used this history of innovation to become a leading manufacturer of not only various floor cleaners, but also all kinds of goods in a number of very disparate industries. As competition increased and manufacturing was a less and less profitable

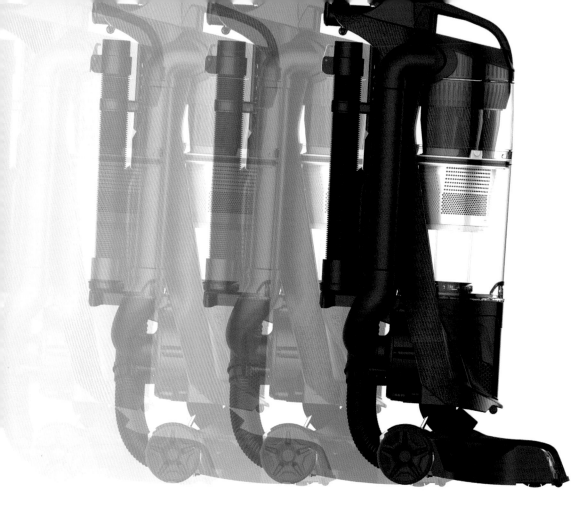

business, Bissell needed a new focus. It became clear that there needed to be a bigger story to tell. Looking at Bissell's DNA—the history of the company—it was clear that Bissell was not just a manufacturer of quality carpet cleaners, but they were, indeed, the authority on clean.

As a carpet-cleaner manufacturer, Bissell had a limited number of things that it could speak about from a point of authority—a limited number of things that it could claim and, more importantly, sell. As the authority on clean, however, they could produce cleaning supplies for anywhere in the home; they could give cleaning advice and helpful tips; they could be the most essential part of any consumer's cleaning regimen. This switch in attitude changed everything for Bissell. Bissell shed all of its business that was unrelated to cleaning, including much of the manufacturing that led their growth throughout the twentieth century. However, within the cleaning industry Bissell expanded beyond vacuums into other cleaning products and tools. Bissell even went on to purchase Woolite. This acquisition fit perfectly into a thirty-thousand-foot strategy of owning the position of the authority on clean.

We often say that "the dream can be bigger than the thing," and Bissell's change of perspective is a perfect example of this principle. The thing here is vacuums; the dream is the authority on clean. What is your brand's dream? Are you an authority on a subject? Do you own a subject area like Build-A-Bear Workshop owns friendship? The "thing"—your product, your service, your retail space, your restaurant—should not be a limiting factor; it should be a springboard to the dream.

> the dream can be bigger than the thing

All of the preceding examples have one thing in common: each brand concentrated on a story— a single unifying theme— that runs like a thread throughout their businesses.

Every decision, whether it be in-store design, packaging, operations, human resources, or any other silo within their businesses, was made with the brand story in mind.

How do you build a brand story for your brand? First, you have to look at your DNA. What is at the emotional and intellectual center of your company? At Build-A-Bear Workshop, it is friendship; at Bissell, it is being the authority on clean. Once you identify the heart of your company, how do you express that story? What are the words and images that tell that story succinctly and with an aesthetic that rings true to your DNA?

The right story can galvanize the crew as well as resonate with your guests.

Club Making

While Groucho Marx famously resigned from the Friar's Club by stating, "I don't want to belong to any club that would have me as a member," it is fair to say the exact opposite is true when creating a brand. Consumers want to be part of a club that they have an opportunity to join. There are many real examples of this. To this day, walking around with Starbucks's mermaid cup makes people feel hip, smart, or in the know. From using Apple products to shopping at Whole Foods to wearing Lululemon, people will always want to belong to clubs. The important thing is to recognize how to create the emotional connection between your brand and the consumer in order to create "clubness."

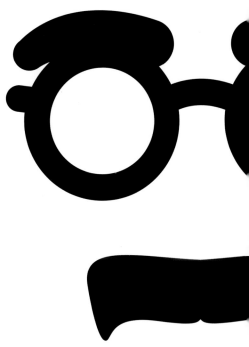

The first step in making a club is deciding what the right kind of club for your brand is. There are many types of clubs. There are clubs that are very exclusive—only the elite can join these clubs.

There are clubs that are inclusive—anyone can join as long as they have a certain attitude or mind-set. There are clubs that are aspirational, clubs that, with a little work, you can join. There are

clubs that are democratic—every voice is heard; every opinion counts. There is not one type of club for each customer. Some people like to be in an exclusive club when they pick an expensive watch, but may want to be part of a democratic club when they are choosing their coffee. You may want to join a gym that feels inclusive but drive a car that is aspirational. Deciding what kind of club you want to be is not about choosing who you want to join your club—it is not about picking a target demographic. It is about creating a feeling that will attract customers and motivate them to join.

Every business has at least two constituents: the customer and the crew. Your club should not only be one that a customer will want to be a member of, but also one that the employees are proud to be members of. Any great brand story, any great club, will appeal to people both in the front of the house, where interactions with the customers take place, and in the back of the house, where the rest of the work gets done. Some businesses have other constituents. Schools, for example, have students, faculty, staff, alumni, and donors. A television station has on-air personalities, off-air employees, viewers, and advertisers. Each one of the constituents must feel like he or she wants to be a part of the club and each one needs the story to speak to him or her.

Following are some great examples of this clubness.

SYRACUSE UNIVERSITY

"The messenger has to be dressed to support the message."

A university is a club in its truest sense. Teenagers strive to become members of the best of these clubs, parents pay for their children to remain members of the club, and alumni carry their club allegiance with them the rest of their lives. Whether schools are competing for the top students, premiere faculty, or charitable donations, clubness is one of the most effective tools that a school can have.

When Syracuse University began $1 billion capital campaign in 2006, they were working with the tag line "Scholarship in

Action." This positioning meant that they did not just teach students in an ivory tower on the hill, but rather they were involved in the community and were affecting real change in the community. This creates a richer educational environment for the students and a better world for the wider community in Syracuse. This was an innovative approach, an idea that the

SYRACUSE UNIVERSITY

INSIGHTS INCITE CHANGE

school believed could be a centerpiece for rallying all of their club members, but they needed to develop a more engaging way of communicating this idea.

"Insights Incite Change" became the new way to describe the concept of "Scholarship in Action." It is an easy thing to say, but the challenge was showing how this was true at Syracuse University. Fortunately, the school did not have to make anything up—a number of remarkable things happened at Syracuse University. Syracuse offered the nation's first bachelor of fine arts degree and had the first African American Heisman Trophy winner. Syracuse University alumni include the first woman to argue in front of the Supreme Court, the first venture capitalist, and the inventor of the first artificial heart. Syracuse has this incredibly rich history of insight and change to draw from. The challenge then became finding a way to communicate this rich history in a fun, friendly voice that would encourage clubness.

The story of the rich history of Syracuse was told through a time line that appeared throughout the school. It was not a time line that looked like it came out of a textbook—it was spirited and bold. The time line became a visual symbol that was applied to the walls of the student union, in the library, on the website, and even on the sides of campus buildings. Looking at this time line reminded students and their parents how proud

they were to be there, and made the alumni and donors feel like they were part of a tradition, a member of an important club. The story of Syracuse was told in a way that made each person, regardless of his or her relationship to the school, part of the club.

The Syracuse story, "Insights Incite Change," coupled with the use of its history, ties the historical strength of the brand to its current forward-thinking approach. By reaching both directions in time, the Syracuse University brand is showing its timelessness. By being timeless, it is appealing to both veteran club members and potential club members. How is your business timeless? Even if you are a new business with no history to speak of, you can find a timeless concept and innovative approach to tie together and appeal to your current and future club members.

metropolitan™
family services

METROPOLITAN™ FAMILY SERVICES

"There is just one story, not a back of the house story and another for the front of the house."

Metropolitan Family Services is Illinois's first chartered nonprofit, and it has been serving families continuously since 1857. Today, it is one of the Chicagoland's largest social services agencies, with over eight hundred employees serving sixty-seven thousand people in 2015. Despite these remarkable facts, MFS has had a relatively low profile in Chicago. Their dilemma: how to go from invisible while in plain sight to the charity of choice for donors.

The place to start is to craft a brand story that is emotional and intellectual. The story would have to express the need they saw, the solutions they were providing, and the impact they had on society. The story needs to address these three aspects of their work in order to speak to the three most important members of their MFS club: the people they help, the people they employ, and the people who provide the money for their extraordinary work. The story also had to be culturally relevant in its tone and look. So many charities have very sad and depressing stories—they try to convince donors to give through guilt. In order to separate itself from the competition, the brand needed to come from a more positive and hopeful point of view.

The first step in creating the brand story was to take their straightforward name—Metropolitan Family Services—and give it meaning through a unique and memorable look. The "M" became the brand story—MFS does not just help families in need; MFS Mpowers them. This story about empowerment, misspelled as it may be, became the filter through which all

families mpowered to lea

communication and positioning was made. The concept of Mpowerment was one that could be used by all of the members of the MFS club. The families receiving assistance from MFS were being Mpowered. The people doing the work in the field— the employees and agents of MFS—were Mpowering those in need. Finally, the people who made it possible for MFS to do its good work were Mpowering the organization by donating.

The idea of Mpowering people rather than "helping" them was a shift of paradigm. The assistance provided by MFS could

rn. to earn. to heal. to grow.

now be thought of as the first step toward independence. This perspective is very motivational for all of the constituents—those receiving the assistance, those providing it, and those donating money to make it possible. Using MPower as the perspective, MFS was able to create a club with a singular message that spoke to all of their members. Each group understood, emotionally and intellectually, that this was not merely charity but Mpowerment.

Who are the constituents in your business? While you may be concentrating on your customer—they are the ones who pay the

to succeed. to heal. to thrive

bills after all—you have to think about who else you need to speak to. In the last two examples, a school and a nonprofit, the targets of the storytelling may be easy to see, but all businesses have a number of constituents to whom the story should speak. A story can speak to not only your customer, but also to the internal team, potential employees, members of the local community, and many other groups. Everyone who touches your brand, even if only in passing or by proximity, is at the receiving end of the poetry and prose that is your brand.

to build. to overcome. to create.

DUNKIN' DONUTS®

"What kind of club are you?"

People are passionate about Dunkin' Donuts coffee. The loyalists, the heavy users who buy the coffee every day, are part of a club that describes their local place as "my Dunkin'." Coffee is a big deal for Dunkin'; they are the second-largest coffee seller in the country, and it is the core of their business. The repositioning of Dunkin' Donuts aimed at two things: first, to stake a claim in the beverage business and, second, to own the "everyman" slot positioned against the more upscale, expensive, and aspirational competitors.

If everyman is going to be the positioning, then you have to make sure that anyone would feel comfortable to be a part of this club. The key art, which is displayed as murals in many locations, is a painting of people of all walks of life walking through the streets with their Dunkin' Donuts coffee cups. This piece of art includes a man in a suit, a mother pushing a baby stroller, a police officer, a musician, and others. The image illustrates that

this club has members of all kinds and everyone is invited to join—the opposite feeling of those upscale, aspirational brands.

Bringing the brand to the everyman is a great strategy, but it has to still feel good for the consumer—the Dunkin' Donuts club member wants to feel like he is a part of a club that he is proud of. To that end, the materials still had to have a modern, hip feel just to reach parity with the competition. Dunkin' was able to create packaging that retained the essence of the brand and leveraged the brand equity but was also a new way of doing things.

When thinking about your brand's club, you have to think about what type of club you want to be. Dunkin' Donuts is a democratic club—one open to everyone. Another position that you could take is to be an exclusive club—one that not everyone can join. Perhaps your club is aspirational—something that anyone can work toward joining. The tone of your club is very important to your brand story. When creating your club, when creating your brand story, you have to consider what kind of club you are. Who would want to join your club, and how should they feel about being a member of your club?

description:

mmmm...
hmmmm

online **education** FOR THE LIFE OF YOUR CAREER

*"it's what you learn
after you know it all
that counts"*

- john wooden

CONTINUED™

"Aim high for 'timeless and universal' when creating your story."

One way to become a club that people want to be a member of is to state that you are the best, the original, the ultimate, or the authority in the area of your business. The tricky business of this is to do it in subtle and smart way. Allied Health Media, one of the nation's largest and oldest online continuing education companies, had made the decision to expand its reach and to offer

its expertise to other sectors beyond the medical industry. Its name no longer fit and its story was too limited, so it had the opportunity to rebrand itself to capture its new strategy. In building a new club, changing the name was not the only opportunity Allied Health Media had. The elements of cultural relevance, modern aesthetics, and smart humor or attitude all had to be aligned—especially in a tech business. In looking for the right name that was in-line with its highest goal of "authority," they went to the source. Allied Health Media changed its name to CONTINUed. The new name literally states the entire

simucase.com
advanced
technology

industry in one term: continuing education. This name and its imbedded meaning sit as the ultimate choice. The brevity of the single term is smart and modern, and the graphics are minimal and clean, putting it in the same visual vocabulary as the world-class brands in the tech world.

To continue the club making, they introduced quotes about education from a variety of sources, from the ridiculous to the sublime, from B. B. King saying, "The beautiful thing about learning is that no one can take it away from you," to the much-loved and respected coach John Wooden saying, "It is what you learn after you know it all that counts." Including these serious to not-so-serious quotes offers a tone that is hip and lighthearted, creating the type of club that they wanted to be. As part of making its club, CONTINUed decided to own a color and a shape. The red square is the visual moniker that marks everything they project. From this square, the brand built itself a literal clubhouse. It took the red square, made it three dimensional, and developed its trade-show booth so potential club members might enter the physical brand's expression.

When building your club, it is powerful to think of how the story can express itself in 360 degrees. A color or colors, a specific shape, or affiliating with aspirational, inspirational, or humorous figures, fictional or real, all can be elements that solidify the feeling of clubness. It is the right brain, or the emotional images or words, that help a person think, "Aahhhh, I feel good around this." Create elements in the experience of your business that the guest or patient or customer can identify with. These are the doors into the clubhouse.

It is not one $6 million idea that you are looking for; it is six million small ideas that build on each other that create your unique brand experience.

getGo

"get in. get out. get going."

The convenience-store industry has gone through a revolution over the last decade. Many of the major chains have improved their offerings and their environments.

CAFE + MARKET

However, to truly move the consumer from a long-held understanding of an industry to a bold, new vision requires both a shift in what is being sold as well as how it is being offered. There also is the possible danger of alienating existing customers by evolving past them. In the C-store business, there are very loyal customers who visit multiple times a day who are very sensitive to any changes. So in implementing a bold, new strategy of upgrading the food and beverages and creating a new guest experience, it is very important to take the customer with you as you change.

GetGo is such a club. GetGo is expanding rapidly and is growing its two hundred locations. It has made the big shifts in quality foods, fresh baked goods, and innovative beverage offerings. The GetGo stores are modern, spirited, exciting retail spaces. But what makes it a club?

It starts with the name: GetGo. The name itself answers the most important question every customer inherently asks: *What's in it for me?* A person is more likely to join a club that targets his or her needs in a direct way than join one that buries its message. GetGo's name is the promise of getting what you need in an easy way. The shorthand, casual nature of the name is also a more modern way to talk to the guest.

The GetGo story is the next part of club making. It is the invitation to the brand:

get fresh. get lunch. get dinner.
get it right. get satisfied.
get in. get out. get going.

Now that the guests have been invited in, it is time to make them feel valued. One way to do that is to give them an identity that they can feel good about. At GetGo the customers are

"Go Getters." Go Getters represent the dual message of ambition in life as well as having a busy lifestyle that requires easy access to the things they need. The Go Getter story is told throughout the experience on packaging, wall graphics, and even in the restroom with a sign saying, "If you Gotta Go!"

There are two main things to learn from GetGo. One, do not aim low and underestimate the guest. Build your club with the most spirited communication. Do not be afraid of humor or attitude, which will communicate with the customer in a voice that resonates with him or her. While you may have a target demographic, the best brands have a large umbrella that many people can proudly stand under. Two, it is powerful to

dignify the membership. Do not be afraid of giving your club members names. At GetGo, they are Go Getters; at LYFE Kitchen, they are Lyfers; at Generate Web Design, they are creative Generators. It is like giving your club members a badge to wear—it puts your customers on the inside of your brand.

Club making is intimately associated with creating a brand story. Syracuse's story is about being part of a club, which has a remarkable history and a forward-looking stance. Dunkin' Donuts's club is about the everyday, hardworking person on the street. Building a club is a natural extension of telling a great story. If you can create a great brand story with a clear position, then people will want to associate with your brand and join your club. Once that association is built, cultivating the feeling of "clubness" is in the details. What are the little things that you can do that reinforce the association with the customer and make them proud to be part of that club? As stated above, it could be naming your club members. It could be providing your club members with benefits or an actual membership. It is in the details; that is where the guest crosses from mere association to a desire to belong to the club.

Country Building

Make "discover and delight" your mantra.

When you travel to foreign places, you expect to experience something new. Often it is a new language. Sometimes it is a new kind of clothing or food or transportation. When you travel, you have a transformational experience. This is the bar for world-class brands—to create a customer experience that involves language, customs, or rituals that are unique and ownable. As your customers step into your store or restaurant, navigate your website, or open your marketing materials, you want them to feel as if they are stepping into a unique world of your creation.

A brand can create a country by developing a unique way of doing things. You have the opportunity to design "discover-and-delight" moments for your guest or client or customer. Often it will not even require doing something new. It may only require naming something you are already doing and taking credit for it. Everything matters—if you do nothing about the look of the restroom, it is not a neutral; it is saying that someone did not care. Make every decision with intention; make every decision your own.

When thinking about creating a country, you can think about what it is like when you travel abroad. How the big things are unique—like which side of the road you drive on, the currency you use, or when and how people eat their meals. Little things are unique as well—the customs of how and when you pay for a meal; the various names for familiar foods, elevators, or bathrooms; and even hailing a cab can differ from country to country. Think about that when creating your country—think about both the macro-experience and the micro-experience. Creating a country can be done with large-scale, hardscape elements or major signage. Creating a country can also be done in the details—how you label your products, the names of your team member positions, or small rituals throughout the customer experience.

> There is an inverse equation between the size of the joke and the credit you get.

The following examples show how some successful companies have created their own countries.

POPEYES® LOUISIANA KITCHEN

"You make Cajun food?"

Popeyes Louisiana Kitchen has fantastic Cajun food. You may not have known that they are a Cajun restaurant because, until recently, they were not telling anyone. In fact, they have been serving Cajun food for over forty years. The fact that they are a Cajun restaurant provided Popeyes Louisiana Kitchen with a unique opportunity to become a country. The fact that there is an actual, vibrant place that is Cajun Country makes it easier to tell a unique, believable story about the country that is Popeyes Louisiana Kitchen. All they had to do was create their proprietary version of what it means to be Cajun and deliver it to the guest.

The transformational experience of being a guest at Popeyes starts with the double promise of "we do good bayou." This is

a promise of good Cajun food ("good bayou") and a promise of good customer service ("good by you"). When inside a location, the guest is surrounded by beautiful Cajun-style artwork showing a vibrant, fun, and food-filled life. There are dancing chickens with hot-sauce bottles; colorful, happy people making music and dancing; and, of course, food. The art is also full of language like "Kickin' chicken with Big Easy flavor," and "Zydeco to Go-Go." The theme continues on to the uniforms, packaging, and even the music. The goal is to transport the guest into Cajun Country.

While a rich environment like this is a great experience, Popeyes wanted to ensure that it did not alienate the existing customer. It wanted to transport the customer to a new country but not make them feel uncomfortable. Popeyes did this by creating language that, if not understood, would not offend the customer. If you do not know that the "Big Easy" is a nickname for New Orleans, then you just think that the flavors are big and easy. If you don't know that Zydeco is a type of Cajun music, then you just think it is a Cajun-sounding word. The restaurant is a rich experience with new things to experience with each visit.

Popeyes was very successful in taking its customers to its vision of Cajun Country. It was so successful that many of the locations had double-digit increases in sales after installing their new brand story.

Having an actual indigenous culture to borrow from is one strategy for creating a country—perhaps in this context it should be called a colony. Cajun culture is rich in language and music and art, but is not very familiar in other parts of the United States and the world. This gives Popeyes the perfect opportunity to export this rich and vibrant culture to other places and provide an experience that is fun and unique to its customers.

> **Walt Disney said, "Yeah, yeah, I know we are building a theme park. I wanna see the weenie, the thing that one person tells their neighbor."**

five BELOW®

FIVE BELOW®

"Give cheap a chance."

Five Below is a country for tweenagers. There are currently over 350 locations across the United States, and it feels like an exciting and unique country. When a customer crosses into Five Below country, the message that greets them on the threshold is: "ADMISSION FREE—everything else $1 to $5." This is a promise of experience, fun, and being transported into a different and exciting country.

This country has its own look. The store is a landscape of architecture that supports the value ideal. For example, when you cross into Five Below from the street, you first encounter six wheelbarrows on a big, red ramp filled with crazy great $5-or-less products. Nothing says value more than an overflowing wheelbarrow. As you move through the store, you encounter fifty-gallon drums filled with sports balls of all types.

This country also has its own language. This country's voice is snarky and funny, speaking to the customer in a familiar-sounding voice and mixing puns and sayings referencing the cheap prices—"Give Cheap a Chance™"— and the temperature reference in Five

Below—"Freeze Your Assets Off™." The language sneaks in everywhere: on large banners and small shelf strips—"Whatever You've Got Will Buy A Lot™," "Hot Stuff, Cool Prices®." By hiding the language throughout the store, there is more for the customer to discover, something new every time they come

in, allowing the brand to unfold slowly and not give it all away in one visit. They may turn a corner and discover a saying that they had never seen before—"Big Choices, Teeny Prices™."

This country also has its own president. George Washington, a reference to the $1 bill, is all over the store. He is also the mascot—appearing on signage, packaging, even on Five Below's annual report. George Washington, as a distorted portrait from the $1 bill, is a reminder of value and fun. While others say that it is all about the Benjamins, at Five Below, they say that it is all about the Washingtons.

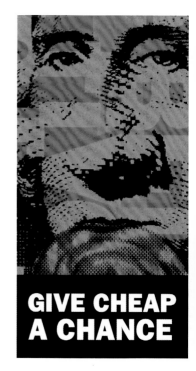

GIVE CHEAP A CHANCE

Every country's language consists of two things: the words you use and the tone in which you use them. Five Below's language has attitude and is filled with puns. What is your country's language? A good first step is looking toward your customer: Who is it? How should they feel when they encounter your brand? With Five Below,

WHATEVER YOU GOT
WILL BUY A LOT

AS CLOSE TO FREE AS IT CAN BE

it is someone young or young at heart who loves to laugh. Your country may have a language that is sophisticated or technical or silly. Once you understand the tone of your country, then you can easily create the actual verbiage that surrounds it.

BUILD-A-BEAR WORKSHOP®

"Where best friends are made."

In 1997, Maxine Clark had an idea: to create a store where kids could build their own stuffed animals. While this idea had the makings of something great, it needed a soul—a timeless, universal, emotional idea to hold this simple idea together. It needed something that would really pull kids into the experience where they would not only enjoy their bears, but truly love their bears. Friendship is a timeless, universal, and emotional idea that no other brand truly owned. A bear can be put away in the closet, can sleep in a drawer, or be played with once and then be simply forgotten. A best friend, however, is someone who has a birthday you remember, someone who you buy presents for, someone who needs a special place in your room and in your life. With this idea as its emotional center, Build-A-Bear Workshop became the place "where best friends are made."

"Where best friends are made" is just the beginning of the story, Build-A-Bear's version of *e pluribus unum* (one out of many), which is the United States's motto that appears on all U.S. currency. In order to really build a great brand, that perspective has to drive all of the creative decisions throughout the business. Build-A-Bear Workshop did this in many ways. Its tenth anniversary celebration was themed "The Year of Friendship"—it was not about celebrating Build-A-Bear Workshop or celebrating the millions of loyal customers; it was about celebrating friendship itself. When Build-A-Bear Workshop sold its hundred millionth animal, it launched a yearlong celebration called "Friends Count," which emphasized the emotional connection between the company and its customers and, more importantly, between the customers and the best friends they created. When your company is celebrating

In naming the separate actions in the process of creating a bear, the entire process itself becomes humanized—adding that little word "me" throughout the experience reminds the customer that they are not just creating a stuffed animal, but that they are also creating a friend.

CHOOSE ME • STUFF ME • STITCH ME
FLUFF ME • DRESS ME • TAKE ME HOME

Customs and rituals are just as important to Build-A-Bear Workshop's status of being a country as its language. At Build-A-Bear Workshop, each bear has a heart, and that heart must be warmed and kissed before it can be placed in your new best friend. Your friend does not just get a name, but you can also give your friend qualities—intelligence, curiosity, humor, love. When you take your best friend home, she doesn't go home in a box or bag—she goes home in her own Cub Condo. These rituals truly set Build-A-Bear Workshops apart; it is not just a retail store; it is experiential retail.

When you look at your brand, ask yourself: What are our unique customs and rituals? If your business is a restaurant, there are many opportunities for customs and rituals to be developed.

If it is a mail-order business, think about your customer's experience when she places the order, when she inquires about the order, when she receives the package. Regardless of your industry, from retail to entertainment to public service, your customer interacts with your brand and there are many opportunities to create customs and rituals.

Through all of these examples, you can see that building a country can be done effectively by leveraging unique language and building customs and rituals. While the previous companies and organizations are all brands that have physical spaces, building a unique language and customs and rituals can be done in any brand and in any business. You have the opportunity to call your products and processes something unique. For example, at Starbucks, you order a tall when you want something small. The moment of delivery from you to your consumer can be ritualized. Even the most banal aspects of your operation, whether it is your customer's receipt (paper or virtual), invoices, or a bill of lading, they can be made interesting with an infusion of storytelling. Building a country is in many ways the culmination of the hard work of creating a great story and designing a great club. Building a country

"If you are going to have a story, have a big story or none at all."

—Joseph Campbell

A big story does not need to have big drama, but it can instead be rich and unfolding, communicating in many different ways. The most exciting part of a brand experience as a guest, customer, client, patient, or fan is the feeling that somehow someone "gets" me.

Branding is a three-legged stool. Between storytelling, club making, and country building, you create a brand that can stand on its own. If you take away only one thing from reading our book, it should be that as a storyteller, club maker, and country builder, you are doing your best to connect in a rich, comprehensive, BIG way with your audience. When we created these stories, clubs, and countries according to this formula, wonderful results occurred. We have helped connect over one hundred million people with their best friends from

Build-a-Bear Workshop. We have helped make millions of scoops of ice cream more playful. For big results like these, a brand must be something more than a teddy bear, burger, pair of jeans, or sneakers; it must be love.

We receive tremendous satisfaction from the work we do at Adrienne Weiss Corporation. We believe we make the world a slightly better place in our own unique way. If someone sees a mural that has come from our studio or reads a pun or joke on the bottom of a shopping bag that we wrote, and that experience makes that person smile or think or even just pause for a moment, then that is a small mark that we have had on that individual's day, and therefore on the world. Much like the way that building a brand takes the deliberate stacking of one detail upon another detail, the stacking of one tiny moment upon another tiny moment can build up to something big and influential. This is what we love at our company. We love building moments, creating connections, and improving the consumer's everyday experiences.

Equally as important as the consumer's experience is moving the meter for our clients. If our clients did not see results from building their brands, there would be no reason for us to exist

and no opportunity to bring humor, connection, and love to the consumer experience. The science behind business is so advanced that it is hard to gain an operational edge on your competition. For our clients, good food, quality products, or outstanding services are mere table stakes that every business is expected to have—if you can't get your business right in these ways, it will be very difficult to tell a compelling brand story that rings true. Such a brand story is a compelling way to separate your company from your competition and communicate on a different level, to talk to the head *and* the heart at the same time.

As we have stressed throughout this book, the work of being able to connect with your customer on these dual levels is not necessarily complex, but it does take effort. Telling a compelling brand story, creating an inviting club, and building an exciting country can be done by any brand if it is a task that you set yourself upon.

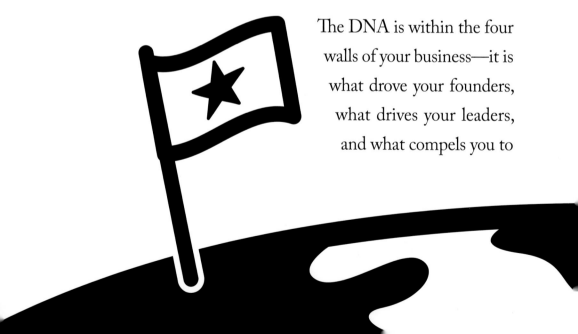

The DNA is within the four walls of your business—it is what drove your founders, what drives your leaders, and what compels you to go to work every day—it is what made you want to read this very book. You can take that DNA and express it throughout your brand experience—all it takes is an understanding of who you are and some creative thought about how to express it.

All that we ask of you is to take the learnings within this book and boldly go forth into your marketplace. Make your customers stop, think, or laugh. Take a look at your business and see how you can communicate to the head and the heart, so you can move your meter. Make your world better, make your business stronger, and make your company's story come to life.

ABOUT THE AUTHORS

ADRIENNE WEISS, founder of Adrienne Weiss Corporation has been called "the high priestess of pop marketing." Since 1986, AWC has been creating award-winning brand strategies for world-class companies from Coca-Cola and McDonalds to Build-A-Bear Workshop, Target Stores, and Disney. Adrienne and her team have created and reenergized brands all over the world.

Prior to the founding of AWC, Adrienne worked with Applause, Inc. to help expand the Smurf brand to over $1 billion dollars in retail revenue. She then became the president of Rage, Inc., a gift manufacturing business. She received her BFA from Syracuse University and did graduate work at American University.

She is an international speaker on brand building. Adrienne has served on the boards of the School of the Art Institute of Chicago, the Gene Siskel Film Center, and the Boys & Girls Clubs of Chicago. She is presently on the board of Metropolitan Family Services.

GREG WEISS is the president of the Adrienne Weiss Corporation. In his position, Greg is a key cog in the creative machinery of AWC, being a part of both the creative and the copy writing teams. Greg also runs the business side of AWC as head lawyer, accountant, and dish washer. He is also the cofounder of FUIR, LLC, an entertainment-focused mobile app company.

Greg has spoken about branding at Chicago's tech start-up hub 1871, the University of Chicago Booth School of Business, and at Kellogg School of Management.

Before joining AWC, Greg attended Johns Hopkins University where he received a BA in Economics. He then earned a JD at the George Washington University Law School. Greg worked as an attorney in the corporate law department of McDermott Will & Emery before deciding to have more fun joining AWC. During his tenure at AWC, Greg received an MBA at Northwestern University's Kellogg School of Management.

simple **truths**®
small books. BIG IMPACT.

CHANGE STARTS WITH **SOMETHING SIMPLE.**

Pick from hundreds of titles at:
SimpleTruths.com

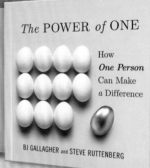

▷ Shop for books on themes like:
teamwork, success, leadership,
customer service, motivation,
and more.

Call us toll-free at **1-800-900-3427**